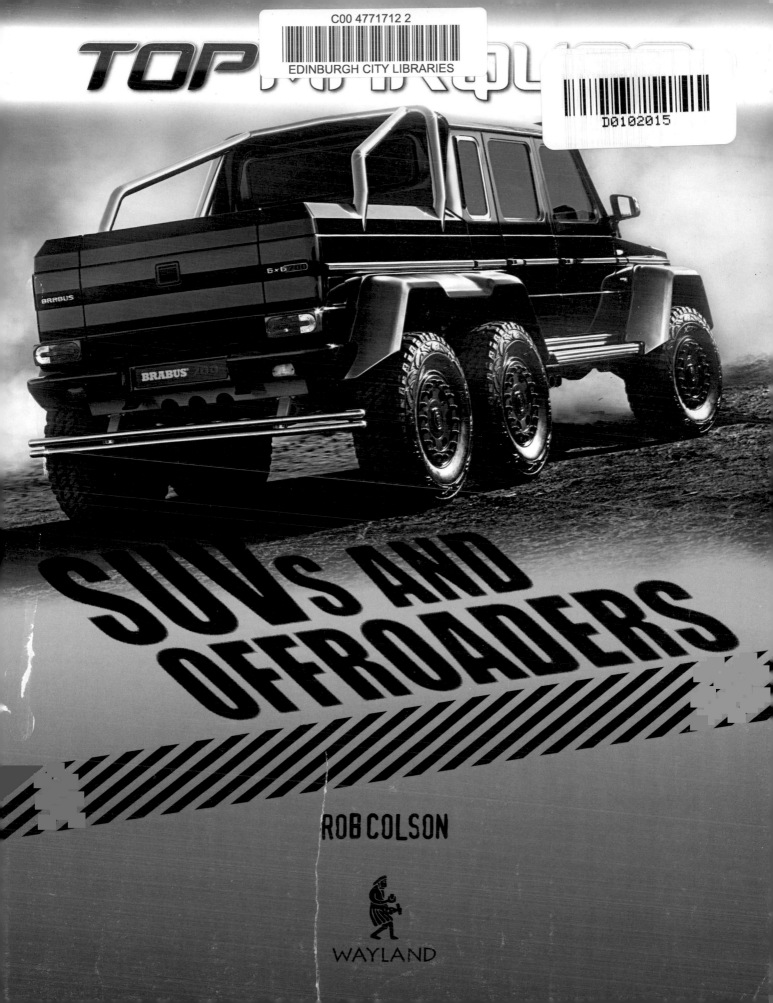

TOP MARQUES

SUVs AND OFFROADERS

ROB COLSON

WAYLAND

First published in 2016 by Wayland
Copyright © Wayland 2016

Wayland, an imprint of
Hachette Children's Group
Part of Hodder & Stoughton
Carmelite House
Victoria Embankment
London EC4Y 0DZ

Editor: Elizabeth Brent

Produced for Wayland by
Tall Tree Ltd
Designed by Jonathan Vipond

ISBN 978 0 7502 9797 4
eBook ISBN 978 0 7502 9478 2
Dewey number: 629.2'042-dc23

10 9 8 7 6 5 4 3 2 1

MIX
Paper from responsible sources
FSC
www.fsc.org   FSC® C104740

Printed in China

An Hachette UK company
www.hachette.co.uk

Please note: the website addresses (URLs) included in this book were valid at the time of going to press. However, because of the nature of the Internet, it is possible that some addresses may have changed, or sites may have changed or closed down since publication. While the author and publishers regret any inconvenience this may cause to the readers, no responsibility for any such changes can be accepted by either the author or the publishers.

Words in bold appear in the glossary.

KEY TO ABBREVIATIONS

MM = millimetre

KM/H = kilometres per hour

HP = horsepower

RPM = revs per minute

CC = cubic centimetre

L/100KM = litres per 100 kilometres

G/KM = grams per kilometre

CONTENTS

The publisher would like to thank the following for their kind permission to reproduce their photographs:

Key: (t) top; (c) centre; (b) bottom; (l) left; (r) right

Front Cover: Stefan Ataman/ Shutterstock.com, Back Cover: Edaldridge/ Dreamstime.com, 1 Brabus, 2 Darren Brode/Shutterstock.com, 3 Porsche AG, 4–5 Snap2Art/Shutterstock. com, 4bl H368k742/Dreamstime.com, 4br Bowler Motorsport, 5b Jaguar Land Rover, 6t Klaus Nahr/Creative Commons Sharealike, 6–7 Michaela Stejskalova/ Shutterstock.com, 7t Jaguar Land Rover, 7b Tony Harrison/Creative Commons Sharealike, 7b Michael Stokes/Shutterstock. com, 8–9, 9t, 9b Porsche AG, 10–11, 11t, 11b Jaguar Land Rover, 12b, 12–13, 13b Nissan, 14–15, 15tl, 15tr, 15c, 15b Toyota (GB) PLC, 16b, 16–17, 17b Mercedes-Benz, 18–19 Edaldridge/ Dreamstime.com, 19t Snap2Art/ Shutterstock.com, 19b Darren Brode/ Shutterstock.com, 20t, 20c, 20b, 21t, 21b Bowler Motorsport, 22l, 22–23, 23t Brabus, 24–25, 24b, 25b GM Company, 26b, 26–27, 27t Mercedes-Benz, 28–29 Christian Vinces/ Shutterstock.com, 28 Christian Vinces/ Shutterstock.com, 29c, 29b Andres Rodriguez/Dreamstime.com, 30 Edaldridge/Dreamstime.com, 31 Bowler Motorsport

WHAT IS AN OFFROADER?

Offroaders are cars that can be driven over rough ground. They have large tyres and long **suspensions** to cope with bumpy surfaces, and are usually all-wheel drive, which stops them getting stuck in mud or snow. Here we take a closer look at a Land Rover Defender.

ENGINE
The engine needs to be powerful enough to push the car up steep slopes or through mud.

SUSPENSION
Suspension rods are attached to the wheels. The rods keep the wheels in contact with the ground when driving over bumps.

EMERGENCY WINCH
Even a powerful car can get into trouble when driving off-road. A winch on the front can be attached to a tree to haul the car out of a sticky situation. The winch is powered by the car's battery.

When driving in remote areas, cars need to carry a range of emergency equipment such as fire extinguishers.

CHASSIS

The chassis is a framework that gives a car its strength. The body panels are attached to the chassis.

MUD GUARDS

Mud guards behind the wheels stop mud from spraying out behind the car.

GEARBOX

Offroaders need a wide range of gears, including very low gears to cope with tough terrain.

WHEELS AND TYRES

Tyres are wide and have deep treads to give maximum grip in slippery conditions.

BRAKES

The car is slowed by pushing brake pads against discs within the wheels.

SUVs

Sports utility vehicles, or **SUVs**, are cars designed to cope well on smooth city streets as well as dirt tracks. SUVs have the all-wheel drive and high clearance of an offroader, but many, such as this Range Rover Evoque, are also fitted out with luxury features to give a comfortable drive.

THE HISTORY OF OFFROADERS

Off-road vehicles were developed in Russia in the 1900s to cope with driving on snow and ice. The first offroaders looked like tanks, with tracks rather than wheels. Later, offroaders with wheels were widely used during World War II. Since then, offroaders have been developed for farmers and other countryside users.

1930–1934

TOP SPEED:
28KM/H

C KÉGRESSE P17

The P17 was a **half-track** vehicle made for the French military. The tracks at the rear gave it the durability of a tank when moving over rough terrain, but the wheels at the front gave it better handling than a fully tracked vehicle. Half-track vehicles such as this were invented by the French designer Adolph Kégresse.

1941–1945

WILLYS

MB JEEP

During World War II, more than 500,000 Jeeps were made for the US Army by Willys and General Motors. The Jeep was lightweight but tough, and played an important role transporting troops over rough terrain. Its name comes from the abbreviation 'GP', which stands for General Purpose. Used at first as a nickname, 'Jeep' was later adopted by Willys as the car's official title.

1971–1985

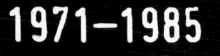

LAND ROVER

SERIES III

One of the most successful offroaders ever made, the Series Land Rover's design was inspired by the Willys Jeep. These multipurpose vehicles were originally designed for farmers. They soon earned a reputation for extreme reliability, and many of them are still going strong decades after they were built.

TOP SPEED:
130KM/H

TOP SPEED:
100 KM/H

1986–1993

LAMBORGHINI

TOP SPEED:
210KM/H

LM002

Better known for their fast sports cars, Lamborghini branched out into offroaders with the LM002. Its durable body was designed to withstand extreme desert heat, and this big car weighed nearly 3 tonnes.

MONSTER TRUCKS

Monster trucks are modified pick-up trucks that have been fitted with giant wheels. These offroaders compete at shows, taking on huge obstacles or crushing cars. The first car-crushing monster truck, called Bigfoot, was made by US trucking enthusiast Bob Chandler in 1975.

PORSCHE

CAYENNE
TURBO

The car is 1.7 metres tall, and the driving position is high above the road.

REAR WHEELS:
480MM

The Cayenne Turbo is a luxury crossover model. It combines the all-wheel-drive durability of an offroader with the comfort of a luxury car and the high-end **performance** of a sports car.

FRONT WHEELS:
480MM

TOP SPEED: 279 KM/H | **0–100 KM/H: 4.5 SECONDS**

ENGINE: 4806 CC | **CYLINDERS:** V8 | **GEARBOX:** 8-SPEED | **TRANSMISSION:** ALL-WHEEL DRIVE

⚙ CUTTING EDGE

The Cayenne offers both performance and comfort. It is fitted with 18-way adjustable leather seats. The driver changes gear using paddles on the sports steering wheel. On long journeys, the car can be set to cruise control mode, which keeps it at a constant speed.

TURBOCHARGED

The Cayenne Turbo is the most powerful model in the Cayenne range. It is fitted with a **turbocharger**, which uses the energy in the **exhaust** gases to add extra power to the engine. Despite being a heavy SUV, the car can overtake on the road as easily as a sports car. It can accelerate from 80 km/h to 120 km/h in just 3 seconds.

The turbocharged engine produces over 100 HP more power than the conventional version.

Front grille allows air over the engine, but protects it from flying debris.

Lights can move to point towards the inside of a bend in the road.

MAXIMUM POWER: 520 HP AT 6000 RPM

SUSPENSION:	BODY:	BRAKES:	FUEL CONSUMPTION:	CO₂ EMISSION:
STEEL SPRINGS	ALUMINIUM AND STEEL	CERAMIC DISCS	11.5 L/100 KM	267 G/KM

LAND ROVER

RANGE ROVER

The SD V8 is the largest and most powerful of Land Rover's Range Rover models. These luxury SUVs are equally at home on the road or on dirt tracks.

Underbody guards protect the steering mechanism from damage.

TOP SPEED: **250** KM/H | 0–100 KM/H: **5.3** SECONDS

ENGINE: **5000** CC

CYLINDERS: **V8**

GEARBOX: **8-SPEED**

TRANSMISSION: **ALL-WHEEL DRIVE**

CUTTING EDGE

The car is fitted with a 'terrain response' system. The system automatically changes the suspension and **transmission** to give the best set-up for the conditions, such as extreme heat or cold, smooth roads or rough tracks. Drivers can also change the terrain response manually on the control panel.

Setting for hot, dry conditions.

Setting for mountain conditions.

Suspension height adjuster.

Setting for icy conditions.

The body is made entirely of aluminium to save weight.

FRONT AND REAR WHEELS: **560 MM**

The suspension is raised on rough ground.

SILK ROUTE

In 2013, three **prototype** Range Rover **hybrids** drove from Great Britain to India along the ancient Silk Route. Over 53 days, the cars were tested to the limit, crossing hot deserts and cold mountain passes along the way. The hybrid is a new model with a **diesel** engine and an electric motor. This was its final test before it went into production.

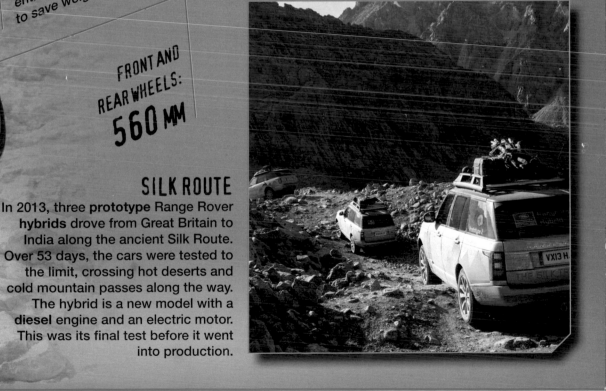

MAXIMUM POWER: 510 HP

SUSPENSION:	BODY:	BRAKES:	FUEL CONSUMPTION:	CO₂ EMISSION:
AIR SUSPENSION	ALUMINIUM	VENTILATED DISCS	12.8L/100KM	299G/KM

NISSAN

NAVARA

The Navara is a pick-up truck, which means that, instead of a boot, it has an open cargo area, or bed. These hard-working offroaders can carry large loads in the bed, and tow other vehicles weighing up to 3 tonnes. The top-of-the-range model is the Outlaw.

The bed is more than 1.5 metres long.

REAR WHEELS: 460 x 180 MM

⚙ CUTTING EDGE

The sun roof opens and closes at the touch of a button.

A touch screen displays satellite navigation information.

The leather seats are heated.

The truck is fitted out with the technology to give a safe ride. The windscreen wipers sense rain, and turn on automatically. A rear camera gives the driver information when parking, allowing them to judge the space more accurately. Inside, a sun roof provides plenty of natural light, and climate controls are divided into two zones.

TOP SPEED: **195** KM/H | 0–100 KM/H: **9.5** SECONDS

ENGINE:	CYLINDERS:	GEARBOX:	TRANSMISSION:
2993 CC	V6	7-SPEED	ALL-WHEEL DRIVE

The roof rack is made from strong tubular aluminium bars.

A large bumper at the front provides plenty of protection.

FRONT WHEELS:
460 x 180 mm

The truck can drive through water up to 450 mm deep.

The bed on a king cab Navara Acenta is 1.8 metres long.

KING CAB

The Navara is available as a double cab truck with four doors and room for five people, or as a 'king cab' with just two doors and room for four people. The king cab version has a longer bed that can carry bigger loads.

MAXIMUM POWER: 230 HP

SUSPENSION:	BODY:	BRAKES:	FUEL CONSUMPTION:	CO₂ EMISSION:
DOUBLE WISHBONE AND RIGID LEAF	STEEL AND ALUMINIUM	VENTILATED DISCS	9.3 L/100 KM	246 G/KM

TOYOTA
LAND CRUISER

A system of fluids gives power steering. At low speeds, the flow of fluid increases to give more assistance.

Hardy and reliable, the Land Cruiser can tackle most off-road conditions. Crawl control keeps the car on course on uneven surfaces, and the car can make it up steep slopes angled at nearly 45 degrees. What the car lacks in speed, it makes up for with the ability to drive on almost any terrain.

FRONT AND REAR WHEELS: 460MM

TOP SPEED: **175** KM/H   0–100 KM/H: **11** SECONDS

ENGINE: 2982 cc

CYLINDERS: 4

GEARBOX: 5-SPEED

TRANSMISSION: ALL-WHEEL DRIVE

FOLDING SEATS

This big car can carry up to seven people in three rows of seats. The two back seats can be removed and the second row folded flat to give lots more room in the boot.

Fold-down rear seats

⚙ CUTTING EDGE

Four exterior cameras are placed around the car to give the driver an all-round view of the terrain. A screen displays a choice of six live images. The driver can switch between images using a control on the steering wheel.

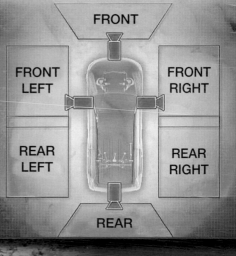

FRONT

FRONT LEFT

FRONT RIGHT

REAR LEFT

REAR RIGHT

REAR

Shock absorbers are constantly adjusted in response to road conditions.

MAXIMUM POWER: 188 HP AT 3000 RPM

SUSPENSION: DOUBLE WISHBONE

BODY: ALUMINIUM/ STEEL

BRAKES: VENTILATED DISCS

FUEL CONSUMPTION: 8.1L/100KM

CO₂ EMISSION: 213G/KM

G-CLASS

The Mercedes-Benz G-Class is a powerful car that is used by more than 60 armed forces around the world for off-road operations. The car has many clever electronic features to keep it moving on difficult roads. Civilian owners can add luxury features to provide a super-comfortable ride.

Heated windscreen defrosts rapidly on cold mornings.

Car can ford water up to 600 mm deep.

FRONT AND REAR WHEELS:
510 x 240 MM

⚙ CUTTING EDGE

A **differential** gear allows the engine to stay connected to all four wheels even when they are spinning at different speeds. The brakes can slow spinning wheels individually, and direct braking power exactly where it is needed. These features combine to help the car to grip the ground in icy conditions or on muddy tracks.

TOP SPEED: **210** KM/H | 0–100 KM/H: **5.4** SECONDS

ENGINE:	CYLINDERS:	GEARBOX:	TRANSMISSION:
5461 cc	V8	7-SPEED	REAR-WHEEL DRIVE

Tough body panels resist corrosion.

The underbody is coated in a layer of plastic to protect it against snow, salt or sand.

Entertainment in the rear seats includes a DVD player.

INTERIOR LUXURIES

Inside, the G-Class is fitted out for comfort. The chassis is engineered to minimize vibrations and noise from the engine, ensuring a smooth, quiet ride. Passengers in the rear seats can sit back and enjoy a DVD on the screen in front of them.

MAXIMUM POWER: 544 HP AT 5500 RPM

SUSPENSION:	BODY:	BRAKES:	FUEL CONSUMPTION:	CO$_2$ EMISSION:
RIGID-AXLE	ALUMINIUM	VENTILATED DISCS	13.8L/100KM	322G/KM

JEEP

WRANGLER RUBICON

The car is 1.8 metres high, giving the driver a good view of the surrounding terrain.

RUBICON

The spare wheel is kept on the back.

FRONT AND REAR WHEELS: 460 x 215 MM

The rugged Wrangler Rubicon can deal with most off-road conditions, whether wading across streams or negotiating rocky deserts. The three-piece roof can be removed, and the rear seats fold away to give maximum storage space.

TOP SPEED: **180** KM/H 0–100 KM/H: **7.6** SECONDS

ENGINE: **3600** CC

CYLINDERS: **V6**

GEARBOX: **5-SPEED**

TRANSMISSION: ALL-WHEEL DRIVE

To cope with extreme conditions, the Rubicon can switch to an off-road setting. In this mode, the gears are ultra-low, providing extra power to the wheels. If a wheel gets stuck, it is automatically locked, and all the power is transferred to the wheels that are still working.

The short overhang at the front and rear of the car allows it to negotiate steep slopes without hitting the ground.

Wide wheel arches protect against splashes.

'BODY-ON-FRAME'

The car's outer body is fixed to a rigid frame, which provides the car's strength. This 'body-on-frame' design makes the car very strong.

The seven-slot front grille is a distinctive Jeep design.

MAXIMUM POWER: 284 HP AT 6400 RPM

SUSPENSION:	BODY:	BRAKES:	FUEL CONSUMPTION:	CO₂ EMISSION:
SOLID AXLE	ALUMINIUM	VENTILATED DISCS	12L/100KM	263G/KM

BOWLER

EXRS

The body is made by Bowler Motorsport, while the engine and chassis come from Land Rover.

Body is shaped to be aerodynamic.

The EXRS is the road-legal version of a car built to compete in cross country rallies. It is made by manufacturers Land Rover and Bowler Motorsport. The car has the same **supercharged** V8 engine as the rally version. It has a low centre of gravity, which makes it very stable.

RALLY CAR

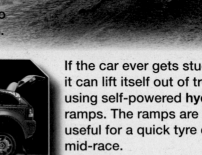

The racing model is called the EXR. It is built for tough competitions such as the Dakar Rally, which means that it has to stand up to extreme conditions.

If the car ever gets stuck, it can lift itself out of trouble using self-powered **hydraulic** ramps. The ramps are also useful for a quick tyre change mid-race.

TOP SPEED: 250 KM/H	0–100 KM/H: 4.2 SECONDS

ENGINE:	CYLINDERS:		GEARBOX:		TRANSMISSION:
5000 cc	V8		6-SPEED		ALL-WHEEL DRIVE

The road-legal version has glass rear windows. The rally version has no rear windows.

Body panels are made from a variety of materials. Where extra strength is needed, carbon fibre is used.

Mud flap

FRONT AND REAR WHEELS: 560 x 305 MM

⚙ CUTTING EDGE

The base chassis is made using a process called hydroforming. Hollow metal tubes are placed in a mould. High-pressure fluid is then pumped into the tubes, causing them to expand and take the shape of the mould. This process allows engineers to form the complex shapes that they have designed on a computer.

Roll cage made of high-strength steel tubes welded together.

Low centre of gravity.

Long suspension for off-road flexibility.

Hydroformed base chassis.

MAXIMUM POWER: 550 HP

SUSPENSION: DOUBLE WISHBONE

BODY: COMPOSITE MATERIALS

BRAKES: VENTILATED DISCS

FUEL CONSUMPTION: 16 L/100 KM

CO₂ EMISSION: 298 G/K..

BRABUS

B63S

The Brabus B63S 700 is a huge offroader specially suited to driving in extreme desert conditions. Its six wheels are all powered by the engine, which shifts its heavy 4-tonne frame with surprising speed.

Carbon-fibre bonnet scoop allows air over the engine to cool it.

⚙ CUTTING EDGE

The Brabus B63S is based on a similar car made by Mercedes-Benz. The Brabus version produces 150 HP more power than the original car, as the engine has been fitted with twin turbochargers. The turbo pipes are coated with gold. This lowers the temperature of the air entering the engine.

TOP SPEED: **160** KM/H | 0–100 KM/H: **7.4 SECONDS**

ENGINE:	CYLINDERS:	GEARBOX:	TRANSMISSION:
5500 cc	V8	6-SPEED	SIX-WHEEL DRIVE

TYRE PRESSURE

A tyre inflation control system displays the tyre pressure, which can be adjusted while on the move. On hard surfaces, a high pressure is best, but when driving over sand or deep snow, pressure may be lowered to give better grip. The car's 940mm tyres are so large that high speeds would risk punctures, so the car is limited to a top speed of 160 km/h.

The car can drive through water up to 1 metre deep.

ALL WHEELS: **585MM**

MAXIMUM POWER: 700 HP AT 5300 RPM

SUSPENSION:	BODY:	BRAKES:	FUEL CONSUMPTION:	CO₂ EMISSION:
STEEL SPRINGS	CARBON FIBRE/ALUMINIUM/ STEEL	VENTILATED DISCS	17L/100 KM	397 G/KM

CHEVROLET
TRAX

The Trax is an SUV that is more likely to be seen on city streets than dirt tracks. This small car does not have the ground clearance for really rough conditions, but it has a turbocharged engine and can easily cope with the snow and ice of a harsh winter.

Solar-control glass stops the inside from overheating.

CUTTING EDGE

The Trax is capable of all-wheel drive, but the car automatically switches to front-wheel drive in good driving conditions. This makes the car more efficient, reserving the extra performance and **fuel consumption** of all-wheel drive for the times it is really needed.

Controls on the steering wheel are operated by the driver's thumbs.

Steering is easier in all-wheel drive mode, which is engaged in poor conditions.

TOP SPEED: **195** KM/H | 0–100 KM/H: **9.8** SECONDS

ENGINE: **1364** cc | CYLINDERS: **4** | GEARBOX: **6-SPEED** | TRANSMISSION: **ALL-WHEEL DRIVE**

Rear sensor monitors the space behind the car when parking.

High wheel arches.

The chunky body is strong and durable.

FRONT AND REAR WHEELS:
405 x 165 MM

MINI SUVS

Small all-wheel drive cars, called mini SUVs, were first made in the 1990s. They were offroaders ideally suited to narrow trails that larger cars would struggle with. These durable little cars proved so popular with road users that manufacturers started producing models, such as the Trax, that are better-suited to roads. SUVs made for the road are known as 'crossover SUVs'.

The car has a lower ground clearance than a true offroader.

MAXIMUM POWER: 138 HP AT 4900 RPM

SUSPENSION: COIL SPRINGS

BODY: ALUMINIUM AND STEEL

BRAKES: VENTILATED DISCS

FUEL CONSUMPTION: 6.9L/100KM

CO_2 EMISSION: 149G/KM

MERCEDES-BENZ

UNIMOG

The Unimog is an all-terrain truck that can be put to many different uses. It is equally at ease going forwards or backwards, and can reach its top speed in reverse. The flexible wheels allow the truck to negotiate boulders up to one metre high.

Driver sits right at the front of the truck, giving excellent visibility.

VERSATILE VEHICLE

Emergency services in remote areas often use Unimogs as fire engines or ambulances. They are also used as snowploughs in alpine areas, in mining and construction, and even to pull broken-down trains.

460mm ground clearance

TOP SPEED: **90** KM/H | 0-90 KM/H: **23** SECONDS

ENGINE: **5100** CC

CYLINDERS: **4**

GEARBOX: **8 FORWARD GEARS**

6 REVERSE GEARS

TRANSMISSION: **ALL-WHEEL DRIVE**

CUTTING EDGE

Wide wing mirrors to see behind the vehicle.

Cargo bed can be adapted for many uses.

The shock absorbers have long springs to keep all the wheels in contact with the ground on uneven surfaces. The front and rear wheels have the same track width. This allows the rear wheels to follow the path that has been compacted by the front wheels.

Tyre pressure is adjusted for different surfaces. High pressure is better on good roads.

FRONT AND REAR WHEELS:
460 x 230MM

MAXIMUM POWER: 231 HP

SUSPENSION:	BODY:	BRAKES:	FUEL CONSUMPTION:	CO₂ EMISSION:
STEEL SPRINGS	STEEL/FIBRE COMPOSITE	VENTILATED DISCS	24L/100KM	N/A

THE DAKAR RALLY

The Dakar Rally is an extreme endurance race that tests rally drivers to the limit. Originally run from Paris, France, to Dakar in Senegal, the race was switched to South America in 2009. Every year, hundreds of competitors take part. Most of the course is off-road, crossing deserts, grasslands and mountains in two weeks of tough racing.

Negotiating steep sand dunes is one of the rally's toughest challenges.

The 2015 route takes drivers through three countries, starting and finishing in the Argentinian capital, Buenos Aires.

TV companies use helicopters to provide coverage of the race, which is broadcast around the world.

STAGE RACE

The course is 8,500 kilometres long. Drivers cover one stage per day. Stages vary in length from short sprints to long treks of up to 900 kilometres. Support teams follow the competitors and help out if they get into trouble. The Dakar Rally is one of the most dangerous races in the world, and many competitors have died on remote stages.

This SMG buggy was custom-built for the Dakar Rally.

Quads have a maximum engine capacity of 900 cc.

Motorbikes have a maximum engine capacity of 450 cc.

TRUCKS AND OTHER CLASSES

Four different classes of vehicle take part in the Dakar Rally: cars, motorcycles, quads and trucks. Many manufacturers use the rally to test new vehicles and demonstrate to customers how tough they are. Other vehicles are completely custom-built for the race. About 80 per cent of the competitors are amateur drivers or riders.

The truck class is for vehicles that weigh more than 3,500 kg. The Petronas team competes in a specially modified Iveco truck.

GLOSSARY

Aerodynamic
Shaped to minimize a force called air resistance when travelling at high speed.

Axle
A rod connected to the wheels of a car.

Carbon fibre
A strong but lightweight modern material.

Chassis
The frame or skeleton of a car to which the car's body and engine are attached.

CO_2 emissions
A measure of the quantity of the gas carbon dioxide that is given off in a car's exhaust fumes. Carbon dioxide is a 'greenhouse gas' that causes global warming.

Corrosion
The gradual destruction of metals when they react with oxygen and moisture in the air.

Cubic centimetre (cc)
A unit of measurement used to describe engine size. There are 1,000 cubic centimetres in a litre.

Cylinder
A chamber in the engine inside which pistons pump up and down to produce power.

Diesel
A fuel that is more economical than petrol.

Differential
A gear that allows the wheels of a vehicle to spin at different speeds from one another.

Exhaust
Waste gases produced by burning fuel in the engine. The exhaust fumes are pushed out of the car through exhaust pipes.

Fuel consumption
The rate at which a car uses fuel. It is measured in units of litres per 100 kilometres.

Gearbox
A system of cogs that transfers power from the engine to the wheels. Low gears give extra power for acceleration or driving over difficult terrain. High gears are used at faster speeds.

Half-track
An off-road vehicle with tracks at the rear instead of wheels.

Horsepower
A measure of the power produced by a vehicle's engine.

Hybrid
A vehicle powered by both a petrol engine and an electric motor.

Hydraulic
Powered by a system of pipes containing pressurized liquid or gas.

Performance

A measure of a car's handling. It includes top speed, acceleration and ease of taking corners.

Prototype

A car made to test a new design. Prototypes are tested before the car goes into production.

Roll cage

A metal frame around the passenger compartment in a car that protects its occupants in a crash.

Satellite navigation

Often abbreviated to 'sat nav', a computer system that uses information from satellites to show drivers where.

Shock absorber

A device that forms part of a car's suspension and smooths out a bumpy ride. Also called a damper.

Supercharge

To force extra air into an engine in order to give it more power.

Suspension

A system of springs and shock absorbers that makes the ride smoother as the wheels pass over bumps in the road.

SUV

Sport utility vehicle. A large car with four-wheel-drive that can be driven on the road and off-road.

Transmission

The system of gears that carries the power of the engine to the wheels.

Turbocharger

A mechanism that uses the flow of exhaust fumes to produce energy. The energy is used to squash air inside the engine, which gives it more power.

✿ **www.topgear.com**
The website of the BBC TV series *Top Gear*, which features reviews of the latest cars, interactive games and clips from the show.

✿ **www.carmagazine.co.uk**
Website of the magazine *Car*, with reviews, videos and photos of a wide range of cars, plus news of upcoming models.

✿ **www.honestjohn.co.uk**
Features on all kinds of cars, with news, reviews and advice.

✿ **www.bowlermotorsport.com**
Website of rally car manufacturer Bowler Motorsport. With information about their cars and features on the rallies they have taken part in around the world.

✿ **www.jeep.co.uk**
Website of offroader manufacturer Jeep, featuring brochures for all their latest models.

✿ **www.landrover.co.uk**
Website of manufacturer Land Rover. Details of all their models, plus features on their latest expeditions.

✿ **www.dakar.com**
Official website of the Dakar Rally, with details of the route for the latest race and photos and videos of past races.

INDEX